# Desert Plants

written by
## Susan Reading

## Facts On File
*New York • Oxford • Sydney*

Published in the United States in 1990
by Facts On File, Inc., 460 Park Avenue South,
New York, NY 10016

**A Templar book**
Devised and produced by The Templar Company plc,
Pippbrook Mill, London Road, Dorking,
Surrey RH4 1JE, Great Britain

For information contact: Facts On File, Inc.,
460 Park Avenue South, New York, NY 10016

**Library of Congress Cataloging-in-Publication Data**

Reading, Susan.
    Desert Plants / Susan Reading.
        p.    cm. -- (Plant life)
    Includes bibliographical references.
    Summary: An examination of the plants that grow in
the desert, and of the specialized methods of water
economy, photosynthesis, and reproduction that allow
them to survive.
    ISBN 0-8160-2421-9
    1. Desert flora--Juvenile literature.   [1. Desert
Plants.]   I. Title.   II. Series.
QK938.D4R43   1990
581.909'54--dc20                              90-31664
                                                   CIP
                                                    AC

Facts On File books are available at special discounts
when purchased in bulk quantities for businesses,
associations, institutions or sales promotions. Please call
our Special Sales Department in New York at
212/683–2244 (dial 800/322–8755 except in NY, AK or HI).

*Notes to Readers*
There are some words in this book that are printed in
**bold** type. An explanation of them is given in the
glossary on page 58.

*Editor* Wendy Madgwick
*Designer* Mike Jolley
*Illustrator* Anne Savage

Color separations by Positive Colour Ltd, Maldon, Essex
Printed and bound by L.E.G.O., Vicenza, Italy

10 9 8 7 6 5 4 3 2 1

# Contents

# What is a Desert?

A desert is a region where the soil is too dry for plants to grow easily. Deserts are found all over the earth's surface and cover about one-third of it. Yet only 5 percent of the world's population live in them.

◄ The Gobi Desert is rocky, with many shallow basins where streams created by occasional short, sharp storms quickly disappear underground.

▲ Sand dunes in the Sahara Desert. Particles of sand are carried along by the wind and piled into heaps that gradually increase in size. The different shapes depend on wind direction. The Sahara has two other types of terrain – the mountains, and the enormous salty flood plains.

Plants, animals and human beings all find it hard to live in a desert, but very few deserts are without life of any kind, for living things can adapt themselves to harsh conditions.

Most people think of a desert as a hot sea of sand. But not all deserts are hot. Cold, rocky deserts are found high up in the mountains, thousands of feet above sea level. The Arctic and Antarctic may also be thought of as deserts because the cold air over them is very dry. However, these regions are not quite the same because in the summer, when the snow has melted, they are covered with mosses, lichens and other plants.

## Hot deserts

Hot deserts such as the Sahara in North Africa have no seasons. The sun beats down each day, raising the temperature as high as 284°F (140°C). However, as there are no clouds to hold in the heat absorbed by the ground during the day, the nights are often cold. They may even reach freezing point in exposed areas. The Sahara is the largest, hottest and driest desert. Dew is the only form of moisture. Animals obtain water from plants and from their prey.

## Cold deserts

Cold deserts such as the Gobi Desert in Mongolia have seasons. In the summer the days are hot, but at night the temperature may fall by as much as 158°F (70°C). In the winter, cold Arctic winds bring freezing conditions that may last for months. Rain falls only in the spring and autumn.

## Water

One feature that all deserts have in common is that they receive very little water – less than 8 inches (20 cm) a year. The rain does not fall evenly all year round, but falls occasionally in violent storms. Vast quantities of water fall quickly. Most of this does not penetrate the sunbaked surface, but runs into river courses, which over the centuries have channeled their way through the rocks. Minerals from the ground have dissolved in these rivers, and when the water dries up or evaporates they are left as hard salty crusts. In many deserts there are underground rivers and lakes, formed by water draining from nearby mountains.

## DESERTS OF THE WORLD

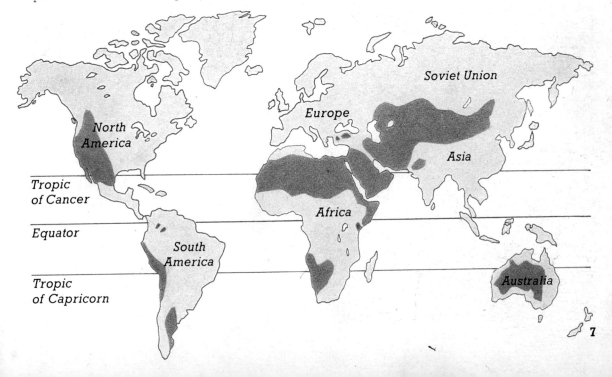

# Deserts of the World

**M**ost of the large deserts are found in the drier parts of the tropics, where the days are always hot. Examples of this kind of desert are the Sahara and Kalahari in Africa and the deserts of Arabia and India.

Deserts also occur in the interiors of continents – in central Asia and Australia, for example – because these regions are beyond the reach of winds bringing moisture from the oceans. Other deserts are found in rain shadows – places that are sheltered from the wet sea winds by broad mountain ranges. Very little rain reaches the Patagonian Desert in South America, for example, because the winds drop all their water on the great mountain ranges to the west.

### North and South American deserts

The Rocky Mountains form a rain barrier to the land lying to the east of them. The high Great Basin merges with Death Valley, where temperatures of 275°F (135°C) have been recorded. Although

▲ *In the Mojave Desert in North America cacti such as cholla often grow in dense clusters.*

less than 2 inches (5 cm) of rain a year falls on this sandy, windswept area, over 600 plant species have been recorded. The most common plants are the Joshua tree and the creosote bush.

Farther south is the Sonoran Desert, where giant cacti abound. East of this, and including the high Mexican plateau, is the Chihuahuan Desert, where prickly pears and the ocotillo shrub are common. To the north, vivid yellow and red sandstones give the Painted Desert its name.

The Patagonian Desert lies between the Pacific Ocean and the Andes Mountains. Cold ocean currents cool the prevailing winds and dry them. This drying process continues when the winds reach the hot land, so no moisture is carried in on them. Cacti and the mesquite bushes are the commonest plants found here.

The Atacama Desert is a high and extremely arid region in northern Chile. Vegetation is very sparse, and in some areas rain has never been recorded.

## Asian deserts

The Asian, Siberian and Caspian deserts run in a belt linking Russia with the Orient.

Here narrow-leaved shrubs such as the black and white wormwoods (*Artemisia maritima* and *A. pauciflora*) are found.

## African deserts

The Sahara Desert runs through the north of Africa to Asia. The Kalahari Desert occupies most of Botswana in the south. The strange *Welwitschia* plant flourishes there (see p. 15).

On the west coast of Africa the Namib Desert has sand dunes towering over 100 feet (30 meters) high. Moisture from night-time fogs blown in from the sea is just enough to support small rock crevice plants such as *Commiphora saxicola* and *Acanthosicyos horrida*.

## Australian deserts

Most of the interior of Australia is very arid semi-desert or desert. The trade winds from the Pacific lose most of their moisture before reaching the Great Dividing Range. The main plants are usually hardy shrubs and spinifex grasses. In the desert valleys, cycads and palms grow, providing shade for smaller plants.

◀ *The Patagonian Desert is a barren, windswept and desolate plateau. It is dissected into blocks by large river valleys that open out on to the Atlantic coastal plain.*

▶ *Mulga scrublands are typical of the Australian desert regions. In this rare photo the pink caper is in flower.*

# How Plants Live

**M**ost plants, no matter where they may live, have to make their own food. The process by which they do this normally takes place in the leaves.

A plant combines water and carbon dioxide from the air in a chemical reaction to form a simple sugar. This reaction requires a lot of energy, and this is obtained from sunlight. Light energy is absorbed and trapped by a green pigment, called **chlorophyll**, which gives plants their color. This process is called **photosynthesis**, and it can be shown by:

Photosynthesis takes place in special structures called **chloroplasts** within the cells. During this process oxygen is released back into the atmosphere. The plant uses the sugars produced to grow. Some sugars will be used quickly, others will be made into more complex starches, or carbohydrates, and stored in the plant for later use.

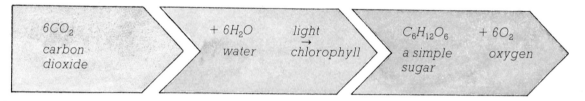

$$6CO_2 \quad + 6H_2O \quad \xrightarrow[chlorophyll]{light} \quad C_6H_{12}O_6 \quad + 6O_2$$

carbon dioxide · water · a simple sugar · oxygen

◄ Only the hardiest plants can grow in the vast rocky deserts of North America. They can only survive where there is enough water and sandy soil for them to root and become established.

► Eucalyptus trees of Australia hang their leaves vertically during the heat of the day to reduce the amount of light they receive.

## Respiration

When the plant needs to use stored carbohydrates these are broken down again into simple sugars in a process known as **respiration**. Oxygen is used for this reaction and carbon dioxide is released.

## The transport system

Some of the water required for photosynthesis will enter the plant through the stomata as moisture from the air. Most, however, will be collected from the soil by the roots. Water has to be transported upwards, whereas food produced in the leaves has to be carried all around the plant. This transportation of food and water is carried out through a network of tubes. These are made up of two different types of cells. Thick-walled xylum cells distribute water and mineral salts around the plant; thinner-walled phloem cells carry food.

## Adapting to light

For most plants in hot deserts, receiving enough light is no problem. Some receive too much light and have to be protected from the sun's rays. Sometimes at the base of the leaf stalk is a swollen area known as the pulvinus, which can twist the leaf according to conditions. Plants in cold desert areas, where the season for growth or day length is shorter, arrange their leaves to receive as much sunlight as possible throughout the day.

▼*During both respiration and photosynthesis carbon dioxide and oxygen are taken into the plant and then released by it. This movement of air takes place through holes in the leaves called* **stomata**. *These holes are surrounded by two very specialized cells known as* **guard cells**, *which can open to allow gas in or out, and close to prevent water from escaping.*

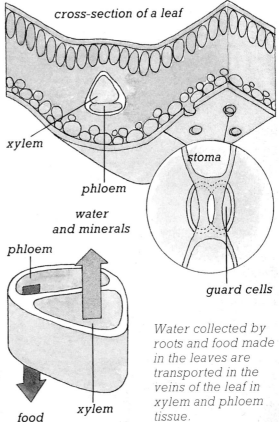

*cross-section of a leaf*

xylem

phloem

stoma

water
and minerals

phloem

guard cells

food

xylem

*Water collected by roots and food made in the leaves are transported in the veins of the leaf in xylem and phloem tissue.*

# Water Balance

**P**lants lose water mostly through their leaves, but also from stems, flowers and fruits. If the amount of water loss exceeds supply, the plant will wilt and eventually die.

Water is taken into a plant by its roots and is drawn upwards as it is lost or **evaporates** from the surface of the leaves. This process is known as **transpiration**. If the air is dry, as it is in a desert, water loss will be high. When the air is moist or humid, much less water will be drawn from the plant. Most of the water absorbed by the plant is lost from it, through the stomata, without it ever taking part in any of the plant's activities.

## Adapting the leaf surface

As water is scarce in the desert, plants have developed many ways of reducing its loss. Most water is lost through the leaves, so many plant adaptations are concerned with reducing the leaf surface. Some plants have reduced it to little more than a flattened stalk, known as a phylloclad. Many plants such as euphorbias and cacti have lost their leaves altogether. In these plants the main body is the stem, which is designed to give maximum bulk with the smallest possible surface area. Photosynthesis, which would normally take place in the leaves, takes place in the modified stem.

To give even further protection against water loss the skin, or epidermis, may be thick, tough and leathery and protected by a covering of wax. The stems also may be protected from evaporation by a layer of spines or hairs, and the stomata may be shielded by lying in grooves or pits.

## Responding to humidity

Many desert plants are able to respond quickly to changes in humidity (the amount of moisture in the air). The stomata only open in the early morning, when the air is moistened by mist or dew, or in the cool of the evening. It has been found that desert plants may lose 6000 times less water than a leafy plant.

In an experiment in Arizona, a large *Echinocactus* was dug up and weighed. It was then left uprooted and without water for six years. When it was reweighed it was found to have lost just 11 lbs (5 kg).

▼Lithops, *or living stones, blend in with their background (top photo). They have roots that can contract and pull the* plant almost entirely underground during periods of severe drought (bottom photo).

## STORING CARBON DIOXIDE

*D*uring photosynthesis and respiration the stomata have to remain open to allow gases in and out of the plant cells. Desert plants may lose more water than they can afford. If the stomata are shut to reduce transpiration, photosynthesis and respiration, and therefore growth, will stop. Some cacti have developed a unique system that allows them to close stomata during the day and open them only at night. Normally this would not be much use, as plants need light for photosynthesis. To overcome this problem cacti collect and store carbon dioxide during the night in the form of an acid. When the sun rises the plant is able to turn this acid into the sugars that it requires. This process has been given the name crassulacean acid metabolism. Cacti can also store the carbon dioxide produced during respiration. It is changed into malic acid and stored for further use.

▼Desert plants save water in different ways. For example, some acacias roll up their leaves during the heat of the day.

▼Grasses such as spinifex roll their long, spear-shaped leaves into a tight straw.

▼The American inkweed loses its leaves during periods of drought. The chlorophyll is transferred to the stem, which becomes green and carries out photosynthesis.

# Absorption of Water

Aplant takes in water and mineral salts through its roots. They also anchor the plant to the ground. The main root, or tap root, runs down into the soil from the main stem. This bears side roots that grow outwards.

The tip of a root is protected by a layer of cells, the root cap. This produces a slimy substance, which protects the growing point (or **meristem**) of the root as it pushes its way downwards through the soil.

## Root hairs

Along each root are small projections called root hairs. These grow into the small spaces between soil particles and soak up water. The drier the conditions the more root hairs are produced. The xylem tubes of roots form a continuous pipeline from the roots to the leaves.

*▲Shrubs like the creosote bush grow several feet apart in the desert to ensure that they can obtain enough water.*

*▼Desert plants have long tap roots or vast spreading, mat-like roots.*

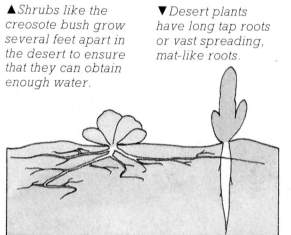

## Deep or surface?

It has been said of the desert that "if it were to be turned upside down and the soil removed it would appear fully inhabited." Although vegetation may be scarce on the surface, the root system required to provide a desert plant with the water it needs is enormous. Some plants like the tamarisk have long roots which extend deep below ground to reach permanent supplies of water. Others have shallow roots which spread over vast areas to soak up as much rain as possible.

▼ *Xerophytes, plants that grow in arid conditions, have root hairs along the entire length of the root.*

▼ *Mesophytes, plants that grow where water is not scarce, have root hairs along only a small part of the root.*

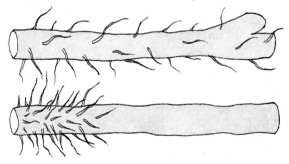

## THE WEIRDEST OF THEM ALL

*One of the strangest plants known to man is found in the Kalahari Desert. This is Welwitschia (Welwitschia mirabilis), named after the German botanist who discovered it. This plant is an unusual conifer, not in any way resembling a pine tree but a distant relative, which has become adapted to life in the desert. It has two very long, tough, leathery wax-coated leaves, borne on a central woody plate. Despite their strength, the leaves usually have a torn, frayed appearance due to the battering they receive from wind-blown sand. They twist and trail along the sand for many feet and are probably the longest leaves known. Running lengthwise inside these leaves, which carry a staggering 22,000 stomata per square centimeter (150,000 per square inch), are channels of very absorbent fibers. These soak up moisture from early morning mists or dews, for it very seldom rains in the Kalahari Desert. When the air is no longer damp the stomata close tightly to prevent water loss. The moisture collected is transported by these spongy fibers to the xylem cells and then to the root below. This root looks like an enormous swollen carrot and can be up to 6 feet (2 meters) across and rise more than 3 feet (1 meter) into the air. Welwitschia is very slow-growing and a large specimen may be thousands of years old.*

# Special Roots

**I**n many deserts there are underground rivers, ponds or springs beneath the surface. Some plants grow extremely long tap roots to make use of this source of water.

Much of the surface of the Nevada Desert is salt-encrusted and barren. Here, however, among the yellow and brown of the rocks, grows the green mesquite bush. This plant can live and grow where no others can survive. Its roots have grown down into the ground – often as far as 100 feet (30 meters) – to reach the underground rivers formed by water running off the Rocky Mountains.

Tamarisk bushes growing in temperate areas will usually have a tap root about 13 feet (4 meters) in length. During the construction of the Suez Canal in arid Egypt, roots of the tamarisk were found at a depth of 55 feet (17 meters).

*Prospis farcta* is a tree found in the area of the Red Sea. It is able to survive because its long tap roots can reach fresh water supplies beneath the salty layers.

The water supply used by these long-rooted plants is far removed from the tiny germinating seedling on the desert surface (see p. 20). Therefore **germination** has to take place during the rainy season, when water is abundant and conditions for growth are good. The root grows extremely rapidly in order to reach a permanent water source as quickly as possible. Growth of the foliage is slow at first, but is made up for later when the roots have reached water.

## Annual plants

Annual, or **ephemeral**, plants have wide spreading roots very close to the soil surface. The plants only grow during a rainy period when much of the water will run off the surface to form small rivers, rather than soaking into the soil.

## Storage organs

Some plants have modified roots which are used to store both food and water. For example, the aerial portion of the Dahlia cactus (*Wilcoxia poselgeri*) is small in relation to the size of the tubers which store food and water. The deerhorn cactus (*Peniocereus*) has water-filled tubers which can weigh up to 44 lbs (20 kg) and are said to have a delicious turnip flavor.

*Ceiba parvifolia*, which grows in Mexico, has miniature round storage vessels attached to its roots. These are filled with spongy tissue that can absorb water. This is why the plant can flower during dry periods when others are resting.

The custard apple tree has a large root over 3 feet (1 meter) in diameter. If the top growth dies the root sends out new shoots.

## Underground networks

The efficient creosote bush relies almost entirely on dew, which only just soaks into the soil. Its water-collecting network is so efficient that no other plants can grow near it. However, as an extra precaution, the roots release inhibitors to prevent other seedlings from developing.

The bean caper is a small, very slow-growing plant – a specimen just 28 inches (70 cm) tall may be as much as 100 to 300 years old. However, the network of roots produced by this plant is enormous. It has been calculated that for 2½ square yards (2 square meters) of plant above ground there will be 42 square yards (35 square meters) of roots.

◀ *The top of a bean caper only grows about ¼ inch (6 mm) a year but its roots grow over a large area.*

▼ *Many plants have developed special roots which store water.*

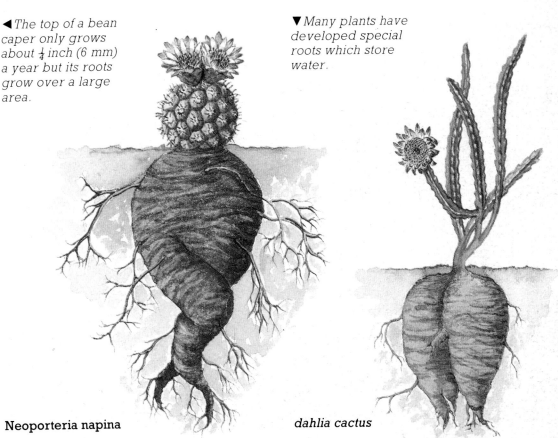

Neoporteria napina

*dahlia cactus*

# Living without Water

**S**ome plants are able to survive after drying out completely without suffering any permanent injury. They survive when conditions become too hot or dry for growth by passing into a resting phase. This can be likened to animals hibernating during unfavorable conditions.

Many of these drought tolerators are found among simpler plants such as fungi, liverworts and mosses. A few of the higher flowering plants can also withstand prolonged drought. They are often known as resurrection plants. During dry periods they show no signs of life at all, but the first few drops of rain will bring them back to life. Within 24 hours of rain, what looked like a dry, dead, shrivelled ball becomes a green living plant once more.

The structure of most drought-tolerant

▲ *The Rose of Sharon of Israel blooms after rain. As it dries out in the sun, the branches shrivel into a tangled ball, protecting the seeds within.*

plants is designed to reduce the loss of water. Unlike many other desert plants they make no attempt to store water for use during a dry period. Some plants protect the leaf surface with a thick waxy coat or a mass of fine hairs. Others reduce the size of the leaf surface from which water is lost. Those with very small leaves are known as **microphyllous** plants. Some plants have no leaves at all (**aphyllous** plants) and their chlorophyll has been "transferred" to other structures – they are called switch plants. The advantage of this is that these other structures have few stomata and are tougher than leaves.

In many desert plants the leaves have become specialized so that water loss is reduced. For example, the leaves of *Colletia armata* are reduced to small green spines. The leaves and flowers of the lambs' tail shrub (*Lachnostachys cliftonii*) are protected by a felty covering, which cuts down water loss.

The leaves of the she-oak (*Casuarina*) of Australia are long and scale-like. The stomata are further protected by being sunken into grooves. This cuts down the rate at which water is lost.

In some Australian shrubs such as the Sydney golden wattle (*Acacia longifolia*) the leaf surface is reduced to just an elongated flattened leaf stalk, or phylloclad. The leaves of butcher's broom are also greatly reduced, and photosynthesis is carried out in specially modified branches called cladodes.

## Creosote bush

Probably one of the most efficient of the drought-tolerant plants is the creosote bush (*Larrea divaricata*). When the conditions are so dry that the bush must pass into a resting phase, the leaves lose their green color and shrivel, but they are not shed by the plant. They stay to protect the small buds that develop beneath them. These buds can withstand drying out, or desiccation, but once rain falls they quickly grow and produce new shoots. The old leaves are then shed.

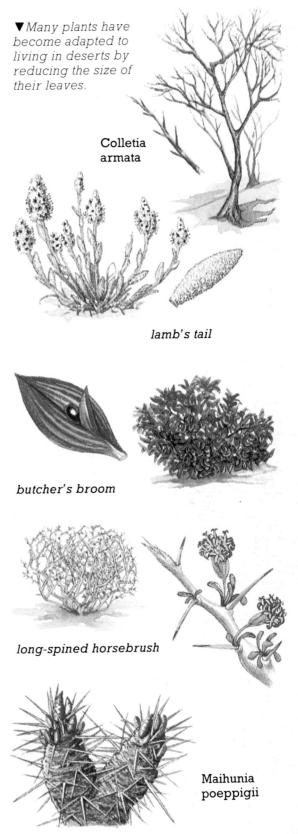

▼ *Many plants have become adapted to living in deserts by reducing the size of their leaves.*

Colletia armata

*lamb's tail*

*butcher's broom*

*long-spined horsebrush*

Maihunia poeppigii

# A Brief Flowering

**T**he arrival of the rains transforms the desert from a bare, dry landscape with just a few scattered cacti and shrubs to a carpet of color. Seedlings push their way up through the sand and within days, leaves and flower buds form.

The flowers bloom and insects, attracted by the scent of the sweet sugary nectar that they produce, arrive. They flit from flower to flower as they feed, and in so doing transfer pollen from one plant to another. This results in the plants being pollinated (see p. 36) so that they can produce the seeds that will, with the next rains, once again transform the desert into a flower garden.

## The desert evaders

These plants cannot tolerate drought or live in desert conditions, as they have no means of surviving as mature plants. Instead, they evade the harsh climate by spending most of their lives as seeds. Only when the weather conditions become favorable and there is enough water for growth will the seeds germinate and grow (see p. 39).

## Sleeping seeds

The seeds of ephemeral plants can remain resting, or **dormant**, in the soil for several years if necessary. Most wild flowers of the desert will only grow after a certain amount of rain has fallen, for a long enough time and during the right season. Moisture such as heavy dewfall soaking

through the soil will not trigger germination – it has to be in the form of heavy rain.

These seeds contain a special chemical called a growth inhibitor in their seed coat, or **testa**. This prevents the seed from growing and only when enough rain has fallen to wash it away can the seed germinate. If too little rain falls or only dew soaks through the soil the growth inhibitor will remain. This makes sure that there is enough water around when the seed develops for it to complete its life cycle.

## Two seasons

Some deserts such as the Colorado Desert of North America have two rainy seasons a year, so there are both summer and winter flowering ephemerals. Seeds of the summer flowers will only germinate if the temperature is above 68°F (20°C). The winter-flowering varieties will sprout at much lower temperatures, and will not germinate until they have been exposed to a long, hot dry season.

*▼ As the length of the rainy season is uncertain, ephemerals must grow and flower quickly before the desert dries out again. One of the record holders for speed is Boerhavia repens of the Sahara Desert. It can sprout, grow, flower and produce mature seeds in just ten days.*

*◄ An Arizonan desert in summer.*

*▶ For a short time not only is there color in the desert, but also the noise of insects and birds. The rains signal the arrival of migratory birds and desert mammals; reptiles and insects mate and produce their young. Here, a grasshopper nymph feeds on the stamens of a cactus flower.*

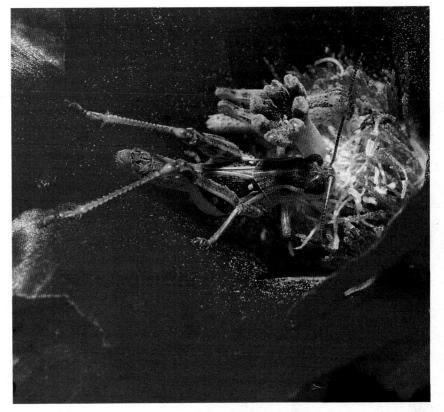

# Surviving Underground

**S**ome desert plants live through dry periods by surviving underground. They spend the short time favorable for growth making as much food as possible, which they store as starches. During periods of drought, the top growth dies back and the plant survives underground.

These food reserves enable the plant to begin growth very rapidly. As soon as rain comes, these organs produce leaves and flowers. Such plants do not store water as they only grow when rain is abundant. These underground storage organs are known as **bulbs**, **corms**, **tubers** or **rhizomes**, depending on which part of the plant is used for storage.

▲ *The desert sage is often found growing on sand dunes.*

▶ *Some bulbs, such as nerines, do not retire below ground. They remain on the desert floor protected from the fierce heat by a thick layer of dead tissue.*

## Flowers in two days

The tuber of the rare west African plant *Chamaegigas intrepidus* is so tiny that it is only just visible to the naked eye. The plant enters a resting phase when the pond it grows in dries up. When a rainy season arrives just a few drops of rain will encourage the plant to sprout. Within one day it will have produced leaves $\frac{1}{2}$ inch (1 cm) long. After another day or two a rosette of leaves surrounding a mauve flower will be floating on the surface of the newly-formed pond. So within days the plant has produced its flower and the leaves are making food which will be stored in the newly-forming tuber. This stored food enables the plant to survive the next season's drought.

## Bulbils

Many grasses that colonize the sand dunes survive drought periods as small bulbs, known as bulbils, which form in the axils of the leaves. The tops of these grasses shrivel, but the green bulbils at the base of the stem are coated in a waxy tissue that protects them from drying out. The desert sage (*Carex pachystilis*) has bulbils that can send out roots within hours of rain. This plant is important in stabilizing sand dunes, for its mass of matted roots binds the sand particles together.

▶ *A bulb is a fleshy swollen leaf base. It acts as a source of food and protects the shoot.*

▶ *A corm is a compressed swollen leaf base. Buds that will produce the next season's growth are found in the axils of the leaves.*

▶ *A tuber consists of either swollen stem tips or swollen roots.*

▶ *A rhizome is an underground stem that bears buds in scaly leaf axils.*

# Storing Water

Rainfall in desert areas may be as high as in temperate regions. The problem for desert inhabitants is that the rain does not come regularly.

The total annual rainfall may occur in a single day as one torrential storm. After this, rain may not fall again for a year or more. Plants must therefore be able to absorb and store water quickly while it is available. Once the water is stored, the plant must be able to retain it for use during the droughts (see p. 16).

Plants that are able to store water are known as **succulents**, for instance cacti and euphorbias, and their leaves or stems are used as storage vessels. These plants have a fleshy appearance, for the bulk of their tissue is made up of special water-storage cells. These large cells are tightly packed together and they contain a slimy substance that draws up water into the cells. The cell walls are elastic, which allows them to stretch and bulge when water is absorbed. As the water is slowly

◄ Many stem cacti have ribbed bodies to help cope with irregular water supplies, while retaining a small surface area to cut down on loss of water through transpiration. The ribs act like a concertina, swelling outwards as the plant fills with water and folding inwards as water is used.

► The trunk of the baobab or elephant tree is very wrinkled. The Australian barrel or bottle tree (Brachychiton rupestre, shown here) also stores water in its trunk.

used up, these walls collapse inwards. They are closely wrapped around the cell contents, ensuring that no air enters, which would have a drying effect.

## Storage in stems

Most cacti are stem succulents. Tall, tree-shaped cacti such as *Pachycereus pringlei* of Mexico, which can grow to 39 feet (12 meters) in height, can collect and store 790 gallons (3000 liters) of water in one day. This enormous volume of water is heavy and may form 90 percent of the weight of the plant. Many larger succulents have a woody supporting network in their stems. When the storage tissue is full of water the plant stands erect. When reserves are depleted the storage tissue shrivels but the woody framework prevents the body of the plant from collapsing.

## Storage in trunks

Tree trunks may also be used as water storage vessels. The baobab (*Adansonia* species) of Australia and Africa can reach a height of 39 feet (12 meters) with a girth of 33 feet (10 meters). The trunk is filled with pulpy matter that holds water. The elephant tree looks most unusual. It has a wrinkled grey bark resembling a skin stretched tightly over the storage trunk. One succulent euphorbia or spurge, has developed into a tree. It has a short stout trunk and a many branched tip.

▼ *Many plants store water in their leaves, and these may range from shrubs with fleshy leaves to tiny bead-like plants.*

*Burrows tail (*Sedum morganianum*), where the stem supports tails of beads.*

*Shrubby mesembry-anthemum of South Africa.*

*A stone mimic (*Lithops*), has just two succulent leaves.*

*The leaves of jelly beans (*Sedum rubrotinctum*) look like globular beads.*

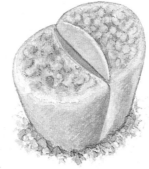

# Plants of the Oasis

Oases are fertile, isolated pockets in deserts where there is water. They may be formed by small springs that provide little more than a waterhole for desert inhabitants, or they may be large enough to support thousands of people.

Oases are usually found in lowland areas where underground waterways are formed by the constant filtering of water from surrounding mountains. The oases of the Colorado and Sonoran Deserts of North America are usually small. They nestle in canyons at the foot of the mountains and are characterized by the native palm *Washingtonia filifera*. One of the largest of these oases, however, has been developed into a large desert retreat, the luxurious Palm Springs.

▲ *If foggaras (wells) are shallow, water may be brought to the surface with buckets. Where the water lies deeper, pulleys and ropes driven by oxen, asses or camels are used.*

One of the largest oases is Damascus in Syria, where 500,000 people live. The river valleys of the Tigris-Euphrates in the Middle East, Hwango-ho or Yellow River of China, and the Amu Darya of central Asia are also oases. The vegetation is lush and luxuriant for periods but the river valleys dry up from time to time. Most oases are much smaller than this and often the water is drawn up by hand from underground wells as in the Gobi Desert.

## Foggaras

In the Sahara there are areas where the underground waters naturally bubble to surface, but often the water has to be brought to the surface from wells or foggaras. The surrounding areas will be irrigated to grow cereals, vegetables, and fruit crops such as lemons, apricots, beans and alfalfa. These will all grow in the shade of the plant so characteristic of the oasis – the date palm. Small oases may support just a few Arab tribesmen or they may be larger settlements to which people travel for weekly market trading.

## Growing crops

Very few American or African oases are untouched by man. Most of the native vegetation, such as the tamarisk, oleander and olives, has been replaced by crops.

▲ *The Salt River Valley of Arizona is a vast oasis that supports the town of Phoenix, where palms, fruit trees and vegetables grow.*

### RELICS OF TIMES PAST

*W*ater filters down from the McDonald Mountain ranges of Central Australia into underground waterways. In places the water comes to the surface forming permanent pools. Australia's past is captured in these isolated oases, which are unaltered by people. Here examples of the animals and plants that would have been found across the whole of Australia thousands of years ago survive and flourish. Cycads, cone-bearing plants, were once the main plant in Australia but now just a few remain. In their shade grow cabbage palms (Livistona), lush grasses, and ferns such as the maidenhead. The pools contain fish that could not possibly have traveled there. They must have remained for generations, along with many unique aquatic insects.

# Keeping Cool

**P**lants of the desert have to cope with dramatic changes in temperature, sometimes from scorching hot to freezing within the space of one day. The sensitive tissues of the plant must be well protected to withstand such changes.

◀ *The bark of the Californian sequoia (shown here) may be 24 inches (60 cm) thick and is almost as fire resistant as asbestos.*

*Trees such as the eucalyptus of Australia shed both leaves and bark to form an insulating layer on the ground. This keeps the roots cool. Many trees have thickened barks to protect the trunks against fires caused by lightning.*

▶ *Some cacti grow close to the ground for protection. For example* Blossfeldia *is the smallest known cactus that grows in ground-hugging clumps amid rocky slopes, and* Pachyphytum oviferum *grows in pebble-like clusters.*

## DEWFALL

*Extremes of temperature result in the formation of dew, an important source of water for desert plants. This can be absorbed by stems or leaves and transported downwards. The roots then release it into the soil, forming a reservoir that the plants can draw on when necessary. Plants that have spines often have them angled downwards so that any moisture condensing on the plant will be directed to the ground, where it can be collected by the roots.*

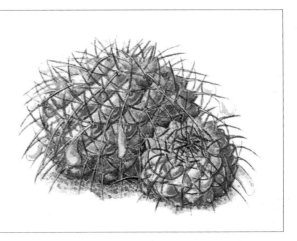

Desert plants are more adapted than others to the sun's rays. Many of them have a white powdery coating of lime deposits over the surface of their leaves and *Welwitschia* has a high concentration of the chemical oxalic acid in its leaves. Most plants have a thick waxy protective coat covered with hairs, which effectively insulates the plant.

## Coping with sunlight

The effect of the sun's rays can be reduced if less sunlight falls on the plant. Many cacti are tall and thin like a column, so that only the tops receive the sun's direct rays. The outer layer, or **cuticle**, is thickened on the side that takes the full force of the sun. In California, for example, this is the southwest side. If these cacti are placed on their sides in the sun they quickly scorch and eventually die.

## Coping with winds

Desert plants often have to cope with vicious winds. To avoid being blown over tall plants must have a firm rooting system. Tall, or tree, cacti initially grow very slowly and only when the rooting system is firmly established will they grow taller. Other cacti reduce the effect of the wind by growing close to the ground where its effects are much less noticeable.

**Blossfeldia**

**Pachyphytum oviferum**

▼ *Large specimens of both* Pilosocereus chrysacenthus *and* Lophocereus *may be 200 to 300 years old.*

**Lophocereus**

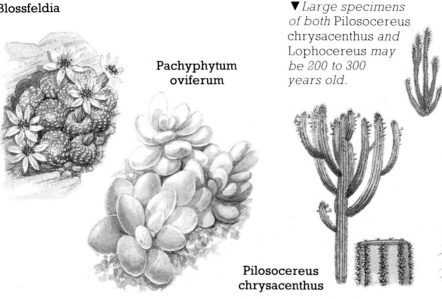

**Pilosocereus chrysacenthus**

# Surviving the Cold

**S**ome deserts are cold for much of the year. These include high-altitude deserts, such as the Gobi Desert in Asia. Others, such as the Great Basin in the western United States and the Patagonian Desert east of the Andes Mountains in South America, are in rain shadow areas (see p.55).

In the Gobi Desert, dry, bitter winds drive in from the Arctic for nine or ten months of the year. During the spring and brief summer months of July and August the temperature may be scorching during the day, but drop by as much as 158°F (70°C) at night. So plant life has to cope with a long cold period followed by a season where the days are hot and the nights very cold. Snow may even fall.

## Adapting to the cold

Many of the structural adaptations of cold desert plants are similar to those found in plants of hot desert regions. They are designed to cope with lack of water. Water may actually be abundant, but it can not be used by plants because it is "locked up" in the form of ice. The cold winds have

▲ *When spring arrives plants that have survived the winter underground, like the wild tulip above, emerge. Their life cycle will be rapid, for they must build up food reserves to be stored underground.*

Anemone patens

**Magenta peony**
(Peonia tenuifolia)

▶ *Grassy tussocks spring to life from bulbils that have lain beneath the ground protected from the cold by a dense mat of last year's dead leaves.*

**Blue grass** (Poa bulbosa)

Ammophila arenaria

**Crested hair grass** (Koeleria cristata)

▶ *Saxouls are also found in cold desert areas. These behave like switch plants, shedding their small leaves when conditions become too cold for growth in order to conserve moisture. Respiration continues through small pores known as lenticils, in the branches.*

**White saxoul** (Arthrophytum persicum)

**Black saxoul** (A. aphyllum)

▼ *Trees are almost non-existent in the wind-swept Gobi Desert. The largest plants are the stunted wormwoods. These narrow-leaved plants are suited to harsh conditions.*

**White wormwood** (Artemisia maritima)

the same drying effect as hot winds. Periods during which growth is possible are intermittent and shortlived. Like hot desert plants, those of cold deserts must be able to respond quickly to favorable growing conditions.

**Black wormwood** (Artemisia pauciflora)

## Ephemeral plants

Cold deserts have ephemeral plants that survive the cold as seeds. These germinate, grow and bloom rapidly when the temperature rises. In a good year up to 40 percent of the Gobi Desert may be covered with ephemerals. Many animals that have spent the winter in underground burrows protected from the cold, emerge and feed on this vegetation to build up the fat reserves that will enable them to survive the next winter.

# Keeping Warm

**P**lants that have to cope with extreme weather conditions must be able to reduce the risk of the cell contents freezing and breaking the cell wall. They must be able to collect and store heat effectively during the day and reduce the rate at which heat is lost from them. Some can even generate their own heat.

As the temperature drops cells may lose water and shrivel. This has a two-fold effect. It concentrates the cell sap and lowers the temperatures at which it will freeze. (This is rather like salting the surface of a road to lower the temperature at which water will freeze.) It also allows room for the cell contents to enlarge or expand on freezing (as all liquids do) without damaging the cell wall. If conditions are dry, it is much easier for the plant to withstand sub-zero temperatures.

## Cushion plants

In cushion plants, the rosette arrangement of leaves in the cushion formation enables the waxy-coated leaves to receive as

◀ *Giant lobelias (Lobelia keniensis) can reach a height of 16 feet (5 meters). The undersides of the leaves are covered with stiff hair-like structures that mat together, trapping an insulating layer of air. At night these long leaves curl inwards to protect the tall body of the plant. During the day they unfurl and the smoother, upper surface of the leaf is then able to photosynthesize.*

▶ *Giant groundsels can grow to over 20 feet (6 meters). During the night their hairy leaves fold protectively around any new shoots. The tall trunk is insulated by a layer of dead leaves, which remain attached to the parent plant.*

much heat as possible during the day. This heat is then retained with the mat. This is effective enough to raise the temperature within the mat to about 50°F (10°C) above that of the surrounding air. These mats often grow in the shelter of a rocky crevice as a further protection against bitter winds.

## Insulation

Insulation against extremes of temperature may be provided by thick waxy cuticles, a layer of dead leaves, a dense mat of hairs, or by the snow itself. Beneath a layer of snow a plant will be kept much warmer than if it were subjected to severe frosts or bitter winds. In the equatorial mountains the plants have to cope with very low rainfall, scorching heat at midday, and below freezing temperatures every night.

## Protection by night and day

Some lobelias secrete a jelly-like fluid into a central cup formed by a rosette arrangement of the leaves. At night a layer of ice forms over the liquid, which does not itself freeze. This fluid protects the leaves and stops them from freezing.

During the day, when the sun beats down and the temperature rises, the ice covering the liquid melts. However, the gel remains and protects the tender innermost leaves from the heat of the sun. It also stops the leaves losing water and drying out.

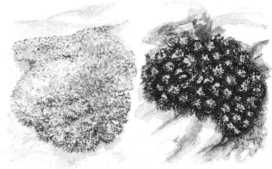

▼ *Vegetable sheep* (Raoulia) *is found in the Patagonian Desert.*

*Golden root nestles among the rocks in the Gobi Desert.*

*Cushion plants trap heat in their leaves.*

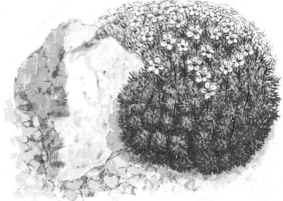

# Living with Salt

**S**alts have accumulated on the surface of some deserts. These salts may form such a thick crust that no plants can grow in the area, or the soil may be just mildly salty. Even so, only very specialized plants, known as **halophytes**, can live there.

If the salt forms a dense crust, roots have difficulty in penetrating it. Even if they do, the soil contains little oxygen.

## Osmosis

The most difficult problem of all is taking in water from the soil, by **osmosis**. Water moves from a weak solution to a more concentrated one through a membrane.

Under normal conditions the cell sap is more concentrated than the soil water. This means that water can enter the plant cells easily. The reverse is true in very salty soils, so the plant will not only have difficulty in drawing water into its cells, but also in preventing water from being drawn out. To overcome this, many halophytes have a highly concentrated cell sap. These cells have large cavities, or

◄ *The tamarisk takes in salty water through its roots. The salts are excreted by special glands, which may contain between two and forty active cells, onto the leaf surface.*

▼ *Artemisia salina does not excrete salt. It is able to prevent salts from entering the plant through its roots.*

## THE SALT BUSH

*O*ne of the commonest salt-pan plants of Australia is the salt bush (Atriplex *species). This plant has to cope not only with salt, but also with intense heat. It does this by reducing the amount of water needed to be taken in by the roots. The leaves are small and waxy to reduce the transpiration rate, and silvery in color to reflect light. They also have a dense covering of hairs, which reduces the drying effect of the wind.* Atriplex dimorphostegia *has bubbles on the under surface of its leaves. At night these fill with dew water, which can then be used by the plant during the day.*

vacuoles, in which the salts collect, so keeping the cell contents less salty.

## Salt pans

Some plants that are not tolerant of salt conditions grow on salt pans. Ephemeral seeds burst into life after a torrential downpour, because this dilutes the salts to an acceptable level. By the time the water has evaporated and the area becomes salty again, the ephemeral plants will have completed their life cycle and produced the next crop of seeds. Other shrubs produce long roots that can tap water reservoirs well below the surface. Their seeds, like those of ephemeral plants, will have germinated and grown when water was abundant.

▼Atriplex hymenelytra, *the desert holly salt bush, grows in the deserts of North America. This white-leaved shrub with glistening rose or pale green tints to the leaves forms one of the desert's spectacular sights. The excreted salt helps to reflect sunlight.*

▶*Many halophytes are succulent. They may store fresh water and excrete salt through glands, or they may be resistant to the toxic effect of salt and store saline water. Pickleweed of North American deserts is one example.*

# Flowers of the Desert

For most of the year the desert looks arid and empty, but when rain comes the ephemerals grow and bloom. Trees, shrubs and succulents flower, and the desert becomes a blaze of color.

These flowers are not produced for man's pleasure – they are a vital part of the plant's life cycle. They are the organs of sexual **reproduction**, which involves the fusion of both male and female cells to form a new offspring. Much of the color and scent is created to attract insects and birds (**pollinators**) to the flower so that the male cells, or **pollen**, can be transported by them to a female cell, or **ovule**, on another flower.

## Parts of a flower

Flowers all have the same basic parts, whether they are from a minute annual or a huge tree. Before a flower opens, its bud is protected by special leaves called

▲*Insects are particularly attracted by yellow, blue and purple. The desert gold* *poppy of California is one of many small annuals that produces flowers of these colors.*

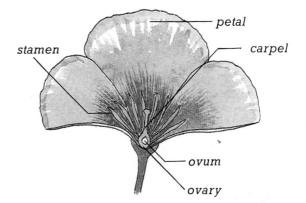

**sepals**. Beneath these are the **petals**, which protect the female and male parts of the flower and attract pollinators. The female part consists of the **carpel**, which is made up of the **ovary**, which contain the ovules, and the **stigma**, which receives the pollen. The male part, the **stamen**, is made

◄*Flowers visited by nocturnal insects often have strong scents. Brightly colored flowers attract day-time pollinators.*

▼*Some flowers, for example* Stapelia variegata, *produce foul smells to attract flies and bats. They often look and smell of rotten meat.*

up of the **anther**, which produces pollen, and a stalk or **filament**. Some flowers, such as the euphorbia family, have colored leaves known as bracts, which often look like petals and increase the size of the flower head.

## Wind-pollinated plants

Plants that rely on the wind to scatter their pollen do not have showy flowers because they have no need to attract pollinators. They have long stamens protruding above the petals, so that the pollen will be blown around. There are not many wind-pollinated plants in the desert because plants are far apart and this method would be too wasteful.

## Pollinators

Insects, moths, butterflies, bats and birds are all attracted to flowers by their shape, color or scent. The form of the flower will depend on the type of pollinator used. Some plants and animals have built up mutually dependent relationships. This means that the pollinator is dependent on the flower for food and the flower is dependent on the pollinator for the dispersal of its pollen. If either partner becomes scarce or endangered then the other is also in danger of dying out.

The food made by the flower is a sweet sugary nectar. It is produced at the base of the petals by groups of special cells, which form a nectary.

# From Seed to Plant

Once pollen has been received on to the stigma of a flower it grows down through the style to the ovum, where the two cells fuse and the seed develops. This seed must then be carried or dispersed away from the parent plant, for if it were to germinate too close by it would be in direct competition for the limited supply of water and nutrients.

Seeds are distributed by wind, water, insects, birds, bats and other animals.

## Wind dispersal

Plants produce very light seeds so that they can be blown well away from the parent plant. Some have developed aids for flight. The Australian caustic bush produces seeds with a feathery parasol. "Tumbleweed" plants dry and curl into a ball around the seed pods. In driving winds they may be uprooted and blown for many miles across the desert.

Many grass seeds behave in a similar way. The sharply-pointed seeds mat

◀ *The bitter desert gourd fruits are produced on stems that shrivel as the dry season sets in. The fruits then break away from the brittle stems and are blown around.*

▶ *Complex seed cases are produced by the South African mesembryan-themums. These remain tightly shut during dry weather but unfold, as the humidity increases, to eject the seeds.*

▼Cereus *cacti*
produce brightly-
colored berries that
are eaten by birds,
which carry the
seeds for long
distances before
excreting them.

together and during their journey around the desert individual seeds break away from the ball. These twist and drill themselves into the sand.

## Water dispersal

The ironwood trees so common in Death Valley produce seeds covered in an extremely hard coat, or **testa**. These are dispersed in the gushing rivers that form after heavy storms and will not germinate until the hard coat is cracked by the pounding waters.

Gushing rivers present *Lithops* with a rare means of dispersal. A small air pocket, formed within the seed coat, enables it to float.

## Animal dispersal

Seeds may be produced in a spiky or sticky seed case that will stick to any passing animal that brushes against it.

Often tempting fruits, like those of *Opuntia*, are produced that contain seeds that are resistant to animals digestive juices. These pass through the animal's gut unharmed and are excreted with the droppings, which provide the young plant with a ready supply of nutrients.

## Germination

During its dispersal, and while waiting for suitable conditions for germination and growth, the seed must be well protected. It is essential to the life cycle of the plant as it contains the embryo which will grow into the next generation of plants. The seed will only germinate when conditions are such that the young seedling stands a good chance of survival.

The seed coat of ephemeral plants contain special growth inhibitors. Only when sufficient rain has fallen to wash these away will the seed start to grow. Seeds of the Australian *Protaeceae* require a period of baking in a fire before they will germinate. The seedling will grow well in the highly nutritious ash.

# New Plants from Old

Aplant must be able to make new young plants for the cycle of life to continue. Desert plants are widely spaced and a suitable partner may not be available for sexual reproduction to take place. Therefore it is common for desert plants to reproduce asexually. Pieces of a parent plant break off and form new plants.

This type of reproduction is known as vegetative reproduction. The disadvantage is that there is no mixing of the characteristics of two parent plants. Each offspring will be exactly the same as its parent. However, the big advantage is that the highly vulnerable seedling stage is eliminated. Often the detached portion will already have an established root system. All plants that reproduce asexually have the ability to quickly form a corky layer to seal the damaged portion. Vegetative reproduction may be the sole means of reproduction or it may take place in addition to sexual reproduction.

## Detachable joints

The teddy bear cholla (*Opuntia bigelovii*) has prickly detachable joints that may be rubbed off by passing animals and carried many miles before dropping in a situation well removed from the parent. Epiphyllous cacti can produce aerial roots from the flattened joints while still attached to the parent. When these are broken off they are ready to grow as soon as they reach soil.

*Sempervivum tectorum* produces completely new plants that remain attached to the parent until they are ready to start an

**Sedum pachyphyllum**

◄*Many plants that colonize sandy regions do so by sending out horizontal roots. New plants grow along the length of the root.*

**Sempervivum tectorum**

Mammillaria

## PARASITES

*The reproductive problems facing desert parasites, which live and feed on other plants, are somewhat different, for they cannot survive without a host. These plants reproduce sexually and form seeds. The seed coats of broomrapes are sensitive to chemicals produced by the roots of the prospective host plant. Without the stimulus of these chemicals the broomrape seeds will not germinate. They are able to remain dormant for many years until they are blown to a site where a host plant is already growing, or until a host germinates and grows beside the dormant seed.*

independent existence. Similarly, *Mammillaria* species produce small new plants on the side of the swollen stem. These drop readily from the parent and will grow into new plants.

*Sedum pachyphyllum* produces thick succulent leaves on a trailing stem. Each of these is able to produce a new plant if removed from the parent during a desert storm. New plants are also made from the leaves of *Calandrinia* species. It has a central rosette of fleshy leaves from which radiate long stems that also bear fleshy leaves. Each leaf, which is often multicolored, can root as it lies on the desert floor.

Should the rooted leaf become detached from the parent plant, it can grow into an independent plant.

### Bulbs, corms and rhizomes

Many of the food storage organs of plants described earlier are also organs of vegetative reproduction. Both bulbs and corms can grow new ones. Underground rhizomes can produce new plants along their length. This creeping habit of underground stems and roots can be seen in many grasses. Their underground network stabilizes sand dunes.

# Protection from Predators

Life in desert situations is hard for plants and their growth rate is slow. As many desert plants are fleshy and store water, they are in great demand as a source of food and water for desert animals. It takes the plants a long time to recover from being heavily grazed, so many desert plants have a means of protection that deters predators.

Many desert plants have some form of prickly defense. Those that do not, very often have chemical deterrents in the form of poisons or unpleasant smells. All cacti possess spines that are produced from modified leaves. Spines help to reduce water loss and the rate of transpiration, as well as giving protection against heat and acting as an aid to dispersal (p. 38). They also act as a protection against predators.

### Thorn bushes

Many trees and shrubs also produce thorns. The camel grass, *Launea arborescens*, is only eaten by the long-tongued camel. Its foliage and leaves are carried inside a barbed ball of spiny leaves supported on a woody stem.

The acacias, or whistling thorns, of East Africa use their armor in an unusual way. Inside the thorns the plant produces a food that attracts ants. The ants bore into the thorns and, having eaten the contents, use the hollows as a home. The tree in return is protected because the ants attack any animal that attempts to graze on the bush.

### Poisonous plants

Poisons are another powerful deterrent. The water stored in a saguaro cactus contains a toxin powerful enough to kill a man should he try to drink it. Other cacti use substances that make them taste so unpleasant that nothing will attempt to eat them. Most euphorbias, the succulent spurges of South Africa, contain a milky latex in their sap, which as well as tasting unpleasant may also be poisonous.

◀*One group of cacti, prickly pears (Opuntia), do not have reduced leaves as prickles. They produce bristles or glochids from a substance called lignin, which is secreted by the plant. These bristles are barbed and if they penetrate the skin they set up an intense irritation.*

▼*Cacti spines rise from small, cushion-like structures known as aerioles, and come in many forms and colors. They range from minute, barely visible hairs to large, tough lethal spikes.*

Copiapoa cinerea *has single spines.*

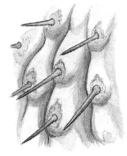

Coryphantha elephantidens *has radiating spines.*

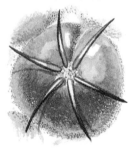

Mammillaria hahniana, *or "old lady," has white feathery growths.*

Ferocactus latispinus *has hooked spines, which have given it the name "devil's tongue."*

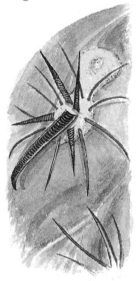

Homalocephala texensis *has been given the name "horse crippler," for its spines are strong enough to pierce the hoof of a horse.*

## POISONED "FRUIT"

*Often poisons are only produced when the rains come. Occasionally some insects will not only be able to tolerate a plant poison but may even use it for their own protection. Sodom apples are so poisonous that only one species of grasshopper can eat them. The poison accumulates in the grasshopper and protects it from being eaten by other predators. Many grasshoppers feed on the fruit of* Opuntia.

# The Succulents

**S**ucculents are a large group of plants that are adapted to desert life. They have all evolved tissues that are modified for water storage, which enable them to survive long periods of drought. Though their solution to the problems of climate is similar, their diversity of form is enormous.

Succulents range in size from the minute to the gigantic, from flattened discs to barrels, from solitary to many-branched columns, from ribbed stem to stems with tubercules.

## Malformations

Sometimes malformations occur in cacti, creating some strange shapes. This often happens when the growing point of the stem, the meristem, where new cells form is damaged. When this happens two or more meristems may form and grow, resulting in monstrous looking cacti.

Alternatively a new meristem may form into one elongated strip that keeps dividing and producing waves of new growth.

This creates cristate forms, some of the most dramatic of which are found in the giant saguaro (*Carnegia gigantea*).

## All Shapes and Sizes

Succulents come in all shapes and sizes. Many forms have furry leaves which help to reduce loss of water by evaporation. For example, *Senecio haworthii* has felty broad leaves growing on semi-erect stems, and *Kalanchoe tomentosa* has upright long furry leaves, which look like rabbit ears. Many succulents have thick fleshy stems and leaves, which store water. Some sedums, for example *Sedum sieboldii*, have flattened leaves on a tree-like stem, and *Euphorbia bupleurifolia* has a trunk rather like a pineapple, with a tuft of narrow leaves on top.

The shape of the leaves also varies enormously between different kinds of succulent. The Mexican *Echeveria gibbiflora* looks like an underwater seaweed, whereas the leaves of *Rochea coccinea* are reduced to stiff sharp prickles, which form a dense covering over the stem.

*◄ Although most cacti have very small leaves which form soft prickles or sharp spines, the shape of the plant varies enormously. The hedgehog cacti* (Melocactus) *shown here grow in the rocky desert of northeast Brazil.*

*▼ Succulents come in all shapes and sizes.*

**Echeveria gibbiflora**

**Rochea coccinea**     **Euphorbia**

**Kalanchoe tomentosa**     **Sedum sieboldii**

## MIMIC PLANTS

*These plants mimic in both shape and colors the red, grey or beige pebbles among which they grow. Their rounded bodies nestle down into the ground with just their flat tops, formed from two swollen leaves, showing. Perhaps this camouflage evolved to protect the plants from predators.*

## Cacti large and small

All cacti are well-adapted to live in the desert. Nearly all of them have thick succulent stems and prickles or spines to keep off browsing animals. But there the similarity ends. Some, like *Cleistocacti*, form slim columns with deep-colored flowers branching from the stem. Others, for example *Copiapoa cinerea*, grow close together in dumpy columns or are many lobed like *Maihuenia peoppigii*, which has peony-like flowers.

Many cacti bear their flowers on the top of the stem. *Melocactus*, for example, has a deep ridge on its crown and the flowers, which grow in a circle, resemble candles on a birthday cake.

**45**

# Plant Partnerships

Some plants form partnerships with other plants. In some cases both plants benefit, and sometimes only one plant benefits from the relationship. A plant that is totally dependent on another for its survival is known as a parasite.

For some parasites the provider, or **host**, must be a specific species; for others a range of plants will suffice. The host may be able to cope reasonably well, providing not only for itself but for the parasite too. However, the burden of the parasite often proves too much for the host, so that it weakens and eventually dies.

## The dodder

The desert dodder grows wherever shrubs are found. Despite the unflattering local name of "devil gut," it is actually quite a pretty plant. It lacks chlorophyll, and therefore cannot photosynthesize. The dodder will attach itself to any desert shrub, although the most frequent hosts are the creosote bush and the bursage. When the dodder seedling first appears, it produces two seedling leaves, but these soon wither. In the meantime, the stem lengthens and winds its way up round the host, producing suckers every time the stem touches a host branch. These suckers penetrate the host tissue to draw

◄ *The dodder is a stem parasite obtaining its food through suckers called* **haustoria** *which link the dodder with the xylem and phloem of the host plant.*

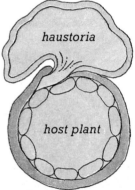

haustoria

host plant

water and nutrients from it. Later each attachment separates from the main stem, forming a new plant that can flower and seed. The host bush then looks as if it is draped in colorless filaments bearing papery yellow clumps of flowers.

## Cooper's broomrape

This plant grows in Death Valley, California. It has no chlorophyll and so has to obtain its food from some other plant, usually the white bursage. Below ground its roots are attached to the roots of the shrub from which it draws food. The only time one knows it is there is when it grows above ground to flower.

## Extra support

Not all plant partnerships are as drastic as these. The dodder and broomrape are complete parasites and without the host they are unable to survive. Others in this harsh environment are able to grow alone but benefit from a little help from other stronger plants.

Some use other plants not for food, but for support. The dahlia cactus (*Wilcoxia*) has fragile top growth. If the delicate stems should break it can reshoot from its underground tuber. When it grows alone it rarely reaches 12 inches (30 cm) in height, but with support from other desert shrubs it is able to grow about three times as high.

The yellow twining snapdragon (*Antirrhinum filipes*) seeks support from shrubs for its flimsy fragile twining stems. The long yellow flowers are a familiar sight among shrubs in the deserts of Arizona.

The desert is a harsh place for seedlings just beginning life. They have no established root system and may easily dry out. The seedlings of the giant saguaro cactus germinate more readily in the shade of the *Palo verdi* tree. Here, shaded from the sun, the seedling will grow. As it grows it absorbs more and more water until eventually the *Palo verdi* will die because there is not enough water for both.

▲ *Some plants use others for support or for shade from the sun.*

▼ *Broomrapes are root parasites. When a seed germinates, a root-like probe penetrates the soil until it finds a host root. The broomrape becomes attached to the host root and develops a tuber. Flowering shoots emerge in summer.*

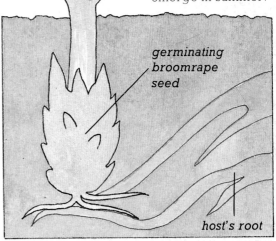

germinating broomrape seed

host's root

# Plants and Animals

**A**nimals do not have the ability to manufacture food – only plants can do this. All animal life is dependent on plants, from the plant eaters themselves (herbivores), to the meat eaters (carnivores) that live on herbivorous animals.

▲ *Both the yucca moth and the yucca gain from their relationship. The yucca plant is assured of pollination and the moth receives food and shelter.*

◄ *Many beetles feed on flowers as well as seeds and fruit.*

In the desert many animals also rely on plants to provide them with water and shelter. The addax, for example, which lives in the Sahara Desert, never drinks. It obtains all its water from the plants it eats. Many desert rodents can only survive because of their ability to collect bulbs. These provide both water and food, and it is not uncommon to find 50 or more bulbs in the underground hole of a desert mole.

## A great partnership

Many plants go to great lengths to attract certain animals, and indeed may not be able to survive without them. Such a close relationship has developed between the Joshua tree (*Yucca brevifolia*) and the moth named after it. The yucca releases a strong scent at night, when the moth is active. The moth, attracted by this scent, enters the flower and climbs up each stamen collecting pollen grains into a ball. This is taken to another flower, where the moth lays its eggs, one in each ovule. The plant provides enough food for both developing caterpillar and seed. The caterpillar (**larva**) leaves the flower and spends its resting (**pupa**) stage in the soil. This may last for one, two or three years, ensuring that if conditions are not favorable for the yucca to flower one year there will be moths for another year.

## Spinifex partners

The spinifex grass of Australia provides both food and shelter for the spinifex pigeon, whose plumage is camouflaged to resemble the grass. Here it will nest, its coloring merging into the background, feeding on the copious quantities of seeds produced by the spinifex grass during the rainy season.

## THE SAGUARO COMMUNITY CENTER

*The giant saguaro cactus is a great provider for desert inhabitants, and indeed some desert animals are only found where the saguaro is abundant. The fruits provide food and moisture for many birds including woodpeckers, pigeons, finches and thrushes. The Galia woodpecker drills into the huge trunk to make a nesting-hole for its young. Insects attracted by the saguaro fruits provide an ample supply of food for the young fledglings. When the young woodpeckers have flown, other birds arrive to use the vacated holes to raise their families. These may be flycatchers, screech-owls or the tiny elf owl. Indeed the elf owl is so dependent on these nesting-holes that it is only found where both woodpeckers and saguaros abound. The vacated holes are also a favorite place for honey bees to build their hives.*

49

# Deserts by Day and Night

**D**uring the heat of the day the desert appears almost devoid of animal life. Animals take refuge in rock crevices or specially built tunnels beneath the sand. At dusk, as the sun wanes, birds, mammals and reptiles emerge from their hiding places.

In North America, kangaroo rats leave the cool of their burrows, where their breath has created a moist atmosphere, to hunt for seeds. These rodents are hunted by the carnivorous kit fox.

In the Sahara, geckos emerge to hunt insects, and gerbils search for any dead vegetation blown in by the winds. These are hunted by the fennec fox. The gerbils quickly get cold but the geckos can generate enough heat to scavenge until dawn.

As the sun rises, the only venomous lizard in North America, the gila monster, slowly emerges. As the day becomes warmer, the lizard becomes more active in its search for insects, birds and any desert mice that may still be around.

▲ *Many insects like this beetle obtain moisture from the juicy fruits of desert plants. They also provide shade and shelter from the baking sun.*

◄ *Desert life during the heat of the day.*

## In the heat of the midday sun

By midday the desert is too hot for all but a very few animals. The ground squirrel of the Kalahari Desert shelters in the shade of its own bushy tail, which it holds over its head. Other animals use small amounts of precious water to cool themselves. When water evaporates from the surface of the skin, it has a cooling effect. Tortoises store their urine and use it to wet their legs or they may wet their heads and necks with saliva. Kangaroos lick their forearms, which have a surface network of blood vessels. The American jack rabbit has large ears that bring blood to the surface to be cooled.

## Following the rains

When rain comes to the desert both plant and animal life is transformed. Animals that have spent months, or even years, as an egg or hibernating come to life. They breed and feed as quickly as possible to build up food reserves, for the plants will soon shrivel and die.

Locusts migrate to areas where rain has just fallen. They feed on the leaves and stems of ephemeral plants. Their eggs, like the seeds of the ephemerals, will lie dormant during the dry season. They will hatch and grow with the next rains.

Following the sudden burst of insect life come migratory birds in search of insects and reptiles. They nest in the foliage-covered shrubs and produce their young.

## Desert frogs

At the first rains the spade foot toad emerges from beneath the ground. The males and females mate and breed very quickly. The eggs are laid in the newly-formed ponds. The tadpoles that hatch one day later feed on small green plants called algae that have developed from spores in the water. As the ponds dry up, many tadpoles die. Their dead remains will dissolve in the water of later ponds to form nitrogen-rich food for the next crop of algae. These algae, in turn, will be devoured by more young tadpoles when the next rains arrive.

◄*Desert life at dusk.*

# Desert Plants and People

**M**any desert tribes are nomadic, traveling from one oasis to the next. They do not settle down and build towns or cities. This is because vegetation is slow-growing and sparse and cannot support large populations.

◄ *The Israel crocus (Colchicum) contains a valuable drug, colchicine, in both its bulbs and leaves. It is now farmed commercially for use in the pharmaceutical industry.*

▼ *Inhabitants of the Namib Desert obtain both food and drink from the desert melon (Citrullus lunatus).*

Desert dwellers are expert botanists; their knowledge of plants is handed down from generation to generation, so that they know which plants are useful and which ones are poisonous. Apart from the occasional hunted animal, or the killing of livestock, plants are the main foods. They also provide fibers for ropes and clothing, medicines for the sick and fodder for the livestock.

## Prickly hedging

In North America the prickly pear is often used as hedging for livestock. Spineless varieties of *Opuntia* are used as cattle fodder. North American Indians are expert at locating the tubers of *Peniocereus gregii* a cactus that stores food and

water in its tubers. It is used as a cure for chest pains and rheumatism, and is also enjoyed for its delicious turnip flavor. The saguaro cactus is also highly prized. Torches are made from the body, the fruits are made into cactus jelly, and the seeds are valued for the oil they contain.

## The date palm

One of the most useful desert plants is the date palm (*Phoenix dactylifera*). This is not a true desert plant, but it is well suited to the oasis because its long flexible trunk can withstand fierce winds and it can tolerate high concentrations of salt. The date palm is nurtured by oasis dwellers.

The highly nutritious fruits are eaten or can be fermented into an alcoholic drink. The date pits are ground and used as cattle fodder. The leaves are used as fuel for ovens, and the fibers can be made into ropes, cloth or matting. The tall straight trunks are used to build homes. The date tree also provides the shade required for crops such as orange and lime trees and vegetables.

## THE THREAT TO CACTI

*C*acti are very slow-growing and an average-sized specimen may be over 100 years old. If any cacti are removed it takes a long time to replace them. Large and spectacular cacti have become very "collectable" and many have been dug up from deserts to be transplanted by collectors or sold in the retail trade. Often they fail to transplant successfully. This removal of cacti can have a very destructive effect on the desert and now, particularly in North America, these plants are protected.*

▼ There is an old Arab saying that claims that the date palm has as many uses as there are days in the year.

# Natural Deserts

At one time there were no large deserts on Earth. The Sahara, the deserts of North America, the Asian desert belt and the interior of Australia were once covered in forests. Fossilized trees have been found in the Sahara that would not be able to grow there now.

In Asia, ruined cities have been found that must have centered around water supplies that no longer exist today. As we have already seen (see p. 27), odd pockets of ancient cycads and ferns have been found in Australia. Other important evidence of previous flora of desert areas comes from pollen grains that have been preserved for centuries. Present-day desert plants such as cacti are a relatively new group that has gradually adapted to

▲ *Tropical deserts form because rain is carried away to other areas. The ruins of many cities, such as Ma'rib in North Yemen, have been discovered.*

more arid conditions. They have been in existence for less than 25,000 years, and so there are no fossil records of them.

## How did deserts form?

Most large arid belts lie between latitudes 15° and 35° north and south, and the deserts of the north are mirrored by deserts in the south. The North African Sahara Desert is matched with the South African Kalahari Desert. The Sonoran and Mojave Deserts of North America are matched with the South American Patagonian Desert. The Asian desert band is matched by the semi-desert and desert lands of Australia.

Distinct bands of arid areas are caused by currents of hot air that rise in the region of the equator. Hot air can carry more moisture than cold, so the air that rises from the equator is hot and moist. As this cools the moisture condenses to form clouds, which release their rain, as they move away north and south of the equator, over the tropics. The remaining cool, dry air is pushed downwards by the flow of warmer, moister air flowing in behind it. This air returns towards the equator, absorbing any remaining moisture on the way. Thus bands of wet, humid tropical areas to the north and south of the equator are succeeded by bands of very arid desert conditions.

## CAVE PAINTINGS

*O*ne of the strangest discoveries made in the Sahara were paintings in caves and on rock faces of large animals such as elephants, giraffes and hippopotamuses, as well as men with their domestic cattle. For this area to have been able to support such a large population of animals there must have been a considerable amount of vegetation. Old tools, carved from ostrich shells, have also been found, indicating that this large bird once roamed freely. Scientists have estimated that the paintings and tools are about 5000 years old.

▼ *Land that lies in rain shadow areas will form deserts. Mountains form a barrier to moist air from the sea. Water is shed on the windward side of the mountains, leaving the other side dry and barren.*

# The Expanding Deserts

The deserts of the world are growing larger. Areas south of the Sahara in the Sahel belt, which includes Chad, Somalia and Senegal, are becoming more arid, receiving less and less rainfall and even going for years without any at all. Parts of India that were green and fertile less than 100 years ago are now becoming barren. This is causing famine for the people who live there.

Between the Sahara Desert in the north and the tropical rainforest in the south is a semi-arid area of savanna grassland. The population in this area is increasing as the desert grows. The trees are cut down for timber and the grassland is grazed so heavily that it cannot recover.

In other areas, parts of the tropical rain forests, where growth is luxurious and rainfall is high, are being cut down to provide more land for agriculture. These areas might seem very fertile because of the lush vegetation, but once the trees are removed there is nothing left to protect

▲ Once grass is removed from savanna or semi-desert regions there is nothing to bind the topsoil, which is then easily blown or washed away. Regrowth of grass in these areas is very poor but thorn bushes and cacti often become established.

◄ Many deserts like this one in Morocco are being reclaimed and used to grow much-needed crops.

the soil. The land quickly becomes barren, as the soil is washed away.

The discovery of oil in places such as Alaska and the Sahara has resulted in many more people moving into these areas. As a result the delicate balance that exists between the native tribes and the animals and plants that support them is becoming unbalanced.

## Reclaiming the deserts

Places that receive a relatively high rainfall can still become desertified if they are overgrazed, but this process can be halted and the original vegetation will eventually return. Where rainfall is low, it is much more difficult for these areas to re-establish themselves.

Attempts have been made to make arid regions fertile again by bringing water into the area. In some places this has been done by pumping water up from underground lakes, that have lain beneath the surface for centuries. This is a fairly short-term solution, for there will be no water to refill these lakes when they have gone.

## Salt pans

In other areas, fresh water has been pumped from outside using vast irrigation schemes. This brings temporary advantages, but many areas are soon turned into vast salt pans. With no trees to protect the soil from scorching heat the rate of evaporation is high and salts that are dissolved from the soil are left behind as a solid, impenetrable crust. Attempts are now being made to reclaim salt areas formed as a result of faulty irrigation by growing halophytic plants which deplete the amount of salt in the soil.

Measures to reclaim deserts are going on all the time. The most effective solution to the problem of expanding deserts is to take care of the existing plants and animals, and to prevent any further destruction of tropical forests and grasslands.

◀ *Artesian wells are sunk to provide much needed water. The water is often pumped to the surface by machine.*

▼ *Many dams are being built like this one in Chile. They allow the desert to be cultivated.*

# Glossary

**Anther** The tip of the stamen, which contains the male cells or pollen in pollen sacs.

**Aphyllous** Plants that have no leaves at all.

**Bulb** A swollen underground structure. A modified shoot with a shortened stem which is enclosed by fleshy scale-like leaves. Bulbs are both storage organs for food and organs of vegetative reproduction.

**Carpel** The female reproductive organ of flowering plants which consists of an ovary, a style and a stigma.

**Chloroplast** A structure found within the cells of green plants which contains the pigment chlorophyll.

**Chlorophyll** The green pigment, found in algae and higher plants, which traps the energy from sunlight and uses it to make carbohydrates from carbon dioxide gas and water (photosynthesis).

**Corm** A swollen underground stem that persists from year to year. It acts as a food store and new plants grow from small buds that develop from the bulb-like stem.

**Cuticle** A thin, waxy protective layer covering the plant. It is secreted by epidermal cells of the plant and its main function is to prevent excessive water loss.

**Dormant** An inactive or resting stage before growth begins.

**Ephemeral** A plant with a short life cycle. They grow when conditions are favourable and quickly flower and set seed. These seeds will remain dormant until conditions are once again favorable for growth.

**Evaporation** The process by which water is turned into vapor and lost.

**Filament** The stalk that lifts the male anther above the petals.

**Germination** The process by which seeds begin to develop and grow, sending out roots and shoots from seeds.

**Guard cells** Specialized cells on the plant surface (the epidermis) that surround the stomata. They control the opening and closing of these pores.

**Halophyte** A plant that can live and grow in salty soils.

**Haustoria** A sucker-like swelling that some parasitic plants such as dodder develop. These suckers force their way into the host's stem tissue, and food and water pass from the host into the parasite.

**Host** A plant or animal on which parasitic plants or animals live and from which they obtain their food.

**Larva** (plural larvae) A young animal that looks completely different from the adult. Tadpoles are the larvae of frogs and toads.

**Meristem** A part of the plant, usually at the tips of stems or roots where the cells divide giving rise to new plant tissue.

**Mesophyte** A plant that grows in places that receive average amounts of water.

**Microphyllous** Plants having a small leaf.

**Osmosis** The movement of water through a membrane from a weak to a stronger solution.

**Ovary** The female part of the flower situated at the base of the carpel and containing the ovules.

**Ovule** The female cell that develops into a seed after fertilization has taken place.

**Petals** The often brightly colored parts of a flower that surround and protect the carpel and stamen.

**Photosynthesis** The process by which green plants convert carbon dioxide gas and water into sugar using energy obtained from sunlight.

**Pollen** Minute grains produced by higher plants which give rise to the male sex cells.

**Pollination** The act of transferring the male cells (pollen) from the male stamen to the stigma of the female carpel.

**Pollinators** Animals that aid the act of pollination.

**Pupa** A stage that some insects pass through between the immature or larval and adult phases.

**Reproduction** The process by which plants produce new offspring. It may involve male and female cells – sexual reproduction, or may be asexual – vegetative reproduction.

**Respiration** The process by which oxygen is taken from air and used to break down stored carbohydrates to produce energy. During respiration carbon dioxide is released back into the air.

**Rhizome** A swollen underground stem which acts both as a food store and as an organ of vegetative reproduction. New plants grow from small buds.

**Sepals** Leaf-like green segments that enclose and protect the developing flower buds.

**Stamen** The male sexual reproductive part of a flower.

**Stigma** The tip of the style that receives the male pollen.

**Stomata** (singular stoma) A small hole or pore on the plant's surface which allows gases to move into and out of the plant during respiration and photosynthesis. Water also leaves the plant through these pores during transpiration.

**Succulent** A plant that can live in arid locations by using roots, leaves or stems to store water, thus giving them a swollen fleshy appearance.

**Testa** This is a tough hard outer covering, the seed coat, which encloses and protects the seed.

**Transpiration** Loss of water from plants through the stomata due to evaporation.

**Tuber** A swollen underground stem or root which stores food and can also give rise to new plants.

**Xerophyte** A plant that can survive and grow in very dry desert conditions.

# Index

# Further Reading

## Young Adult Books – General

Black, David. *Plants*. New York: Facts On File, 1986.

Forsthoeful, John. *Discovering Botany*. New York: DOK Publishers, 1982.

Lambert, David. *Vegetation*. New York: Franklin Watts, 1984.

## Adult Books – Desert Plants

Dodge, Natt. *One Hundred Desert Wildflowers in Natural Color*. Southwest Parks and Monuments Association, 1963.

MacDougal, Daniel. *Botanical Features of North American Deserts*. Johnson Reprint Organization.

Nabhan, Gary. *Gathering the Desert*. Tuscon: University of Arizona Press, 1985.

## Adult Books – General Reference about Botany

New England Wild Flower Society Staff. *Botany for All Ages*. New Jersey: Globe Pequot Press, 1989.

Rost, Thomas L. Botany: *A Brief Introduction to Plant Biology*. New York: John Willey & Sons, 1984.

Tootill, Elizabeth (ed.). *The Facts On File Dictionary of Botany*. New York: Facts On File, 1984.

---

## Photographic credits

*t* = top, *b* = bottom, *l* = left, *r* = right

Cover: Bruce Coleman; page 6*t* Frank Lane/Silvestris; page 6*b* Frank Lane/Silvestris; page 8*t* Frank Lane/Silvestris; page 8*b* Bruce Coleman/Francisco Erize; page 9 Frank Lane; page 10 Frank Lane/Steve McCutcheon; page 11 Bruce Coleman/Sullivan and Rogers; page 12*t* Bruce Coleman/Frieder Sauer; 12*b* Frank Lane/Premaphotos Wildlife; page 13 Bruce Coleman/John Shaw; page 13 Bruce Coleman/B. and C. Calhoun; page 14 Frank Lane/W. Wisniewski; page 16 Frank Lane/Eric and David Hosking; page 18*r* Bruce Coleman/Denis Green; page 18*l* Frank Lane/Holt Studios; page 20 Bruce Coleman/B. and C. Calhoun; page 21 Frank Lane/Premaphotos Wildlife; page 22 Bruce Coleman/Charlie Ott; page 23 Harry Smith/Polunin Collection; page 24 Frank Lane/M. Newman; page 25 Frank Lane/Premaphotos Wildlife; page 27 Bruce Coleman/Kim Taylor; page 28*t* Audience Planners; page 28*b* Bruce Coleman/Jan Taylor; page 29 Bruce Coleman/Michael Viard; page 30 Bruce Coleman/H. Jungius; page 32 Bruce Coleman/F. Sauer; page 33 Bruce Coleman/Gerald Cubitt; page 34 Frank Lane/Premaphotos Wildlife; page 35 Bruce Coleman/B. and C. Calhoun; page 36 Frank Lane/Premaphotos Wildlife; page 37*l* Frank Lane/N. Cattlin; page 37*r* Frank Lane/Premaphotos Wildlife; page 38 Bruce Coleman/Peter Ward; page 39 Bruce Coleman; page 40 Bruce Coleman/F. Lanting; page 41 Frank Lane/N. Cattlin; page 42 Bruce Coleman/F. Lanting; page 43 Frank Lane/Premaphotos Wildlife; page 44 Bruce Coleman/L.C. Marigo; page 45 Frank Lane/Premaphotos Wildlife; page 46 Bruce Coleman/Charlie Ott; page 48*t* Bruce Coleman/M.P.L. Fogden; page 48*b* Frank Lane/Premaphotos Wildlife; page 50 Bruce Coleman/G.D. Plage; page 52*t* Smith/Polunin Collection; page 52*b* Frank Lane/Premaphotos Wildlife; page 53 Frank Lane/Premaphotos Wildlife; page 54 Frank Lane/Eric and David Hosking; page 55 Bruce Coleman/O. Langrand; page 56*t* Bruce Coleman/Jeff Foot; page 56*b* Frank Lane/Roger Tidman; page 57*l* Frank Lane/Holt Studios; page 57*r* Frank Lane/Premaphotos Wildlife.